Windows 10

The Ultimate Updated User Guide to Microsoft Windows 10 for Advanced Users (2016 updated user guide, tips and tricks, user manual, user guide, Windows 10)

STEVE JACOBS

STEVE JACOBS

Copyright © 2016 Steve Jacobs

All rights reserved.

ISBN: 1537545477

ISBN-13: 978-1537545479

CONTENTS

Introduction 4

Chapter 1: Return of the Start Menu 6

Chapter 2: New Features 8

Chapter 3: Photos 11

Chapter 4: Apps 14

Chapter 5: Quick Guide 18

Chapter 6: Tips & Tricks 23

Chapter 7: How To Repair Common Problems 35

Chapter 8: Windows Update Delivery 55

Chapter 9: Advanced Customizations 59

Conclusion 70

Introduction

Windows 10 is comfortable in the way users know Windows to be: a recognizable Start Menu, synergistic, side-by-side app presentation, and an intuitive new system that is easy to navigate and pleasing to look at.

The *Settings* app, conveniently located in the *Start Menu*, is an entire replacement to the old control panel and it is mighty. With clean lines and an effortless image, the *Settings* menu lets you control, tweak, and toggle everything you need to. We will show you a number of settings you can change using this new app.

Keyboard and other shortcuts are included to enable the user to feel empowered in not only the preparation and update processes but also the introduction to new features and applications that are available with the Windows 10 upgrade. Third-party apps found in the Windows Store now behave the same as the universal apps on a user's PC, tablet, or phone, although some applications may not be able to be fully integrated between platforms at this time.

Windows 10 boasts a great deal of ways that you can customize your operating system with stylish color changing options and the ability to pin and unpin items to the start menu, taskbar, desktop, and more. In this book we will also show you how to personalize the lock screen, change your background image, apply a slideshow, and turn tips and tricks on and off.

As with any piece of technology or operating system the occasional issue is, unfortunately, part of the package. Things are not guaranteed to always go smoothly. But we explain the most common of problems and show you how you can correct them. Microsoft has designed steps that will quickly resolve your issues. Use our step-by-step guides to start your PC in safe mode, fix a host of screen problems, correct any update failures, and more with ease.

Windows 10 comes with the all new Wi-Fi Sense, which is, of course, another feature that you can disable should you wish. But it is a feature that is designed to save you time and give you Internet access in mere seconds. Wi-Fi Sense is able to suggest open hotspots to you and even automatically connect to them. We will explain both the benefits and risks of these features and show you how to change these settings to suit your needs.

Windows 10 is a new and exciting adventure for PC users of all types. Those familiar with older versions will find certain 'creature comforts' that will make them feel right at home, while newer users of Microsoft's operating system will find less frustration and much more function in this clean, beautiful, and friendly version of Windows 10!

Chapter 1: Return of the Start Menu

The Windows 10 start menu is a hybrid of past start-up menus from the 'old days' and the odd start screen that debuted with Windows 8. The new start menu is something that both traditional computer and tablet users will like. The following chapter will familiarize users with the basics.

For those who really disliked the start screen of Windows 8, the user will find that the best parts of the concept have prevailed. Gone is the clunky desktop and tablet start screen with limited customization and confusing presentation. The new start menu is friendly to the user and computer alike.

The familiarity of the new start menu is felt with the first click. The menu pops open, just like in the old days. Different is the ability to resize the start menu—just grab at the top or right edges and drag to the user's preference. The *Personalization* submenu within the new *Settings* folder will allow the user to change more aspects of the start menu. Just click on *Start* to begin personalizing the start menu today. Users can also individualize the start menu to show newly added apps and recently used items in a jump list for easy access.

The start menu can be easily converted for tablet access by selecting the *Use Start Full Screen* option.

The choice of folders that appear in the start menu is also fully customizable by using the *Choose which folders appear on start* link at the bottom of the *Start* options. There is also a very handy *All Apps* link in the same place. This enables access to every program and application installed on the computer.

Another throwback to the old start menu is the power button, which will allow the user to shut down, restart, hibernate, or put the computer to sleep.

Users can also switch accounts, log out, change account settings, or lock the machine with a simple click of the user icon or photo at the top of the start menu! If a user chooses to change the start menu's color, that can be accomplished in the *Personalization* section by selecting the *Color* options.

Chapter 2: New Features

Windows 10 has several new features that add speed, fun, and function to the digital experience. Appearance, synergistic app behavior, assistance, superior browsing capability, intuitive settings and doodling—who can complain with the wide and varied additions to this new operating system?!

Windows 10 introduces the user's newest, smartest, and best friend, Cortana. As a hybrid of Apple's Siri and Google Now, Cortana is fully integrated on both desktop and mobile platforms. For the desktop, however, there are some added features, like real-time dictation for email and inclusion of the hard drive contents when executing searches. Cortana also functions seamlessly within Edge when browsing by default. You can find Cortana's search box in the task bar, type in your question or click/tap the microphone icon next to the search box to enable voice query. To access Cortana's features, use the buttons to the left of the open application window.

Universal Apps is another addition that has brought full integration between phone, tablet, and desktop, even Xbox One. Several of the applications from before have been revamped for this new level of exposure. Those users used to the standard Office Suite will find a totally new Outlook that is in sync with Word to facilitate email display and composition. The Photo app also looks and feels refreshed with editing and album set up that are easy to understand.

Edge, Microsoft's new browser is the biggest new addition for the operating system. Edge is different than its predecessor, with many handy, built-in features like a screen grab tool, touchscreen doodling, notepad, and reading mode. Cortana integration enables directions to a restaurant that you just booked online to be available on a phone or tablet to guide you during the drive. The appearance, tabbed layout, and URL/search bar will feel comfortable to the Internet Explorer user.

Cross-platform apps have been fully updated and work on a computer, phone, tablet, or Xbox One. Windows 8 users will be more familiar with some of these apps if they complete the 8.1 upgrade. The app experience is user-friendly and easy to initiate directly from the apps store. Users can explore the store from the start menu.

The settings menu is a place where basic settings, network, setup, and privacy are centrally located for convenience. The experience is clean and resembles something from Windows 8. The PC settings menu has much more functionality. The new settings menu is prominently displayed on the start menu and is an updated alternative to the classic Windows Control Panel.

Xbox Live and the new Xbox App bring to the table a new format for gaming that is cross-platform and synergistic. The app brings a new experience, allowing the user access to the massive, Xbox Live gaming network no matter what device they are on! Users are able to capture, share, and edit all the highest achievements of their gaming with Game DVR. New games can be initiated across devices with multiple players just as if all were sharing over the gaming console network.

DirectX 12 games will see big improvements in Windows 10 with increased efficiency, speed, and an upgraded graphics package. Xbox Wire is also a new feature that allows direct game streaming within the home across all platforms—desktop, tablet, and Xbox—with ease.

Finally, Continuum mode allows Windows to flow between PC input devices (keyboard and mouse), tablet, touch input, and voice as the operating system detects the transition and intuitively switches to the new input mode being used. Continuum is only available on devices that are currently 2-in-1 enabled.

Chapter 3: Photos

The Photos app creates slideshows, organizes pictures by date, curates albums, and has some good editing features so users can share photos to social media in just a few clicks. While no threat to Photoshop, the new app is impressive and feature rich.

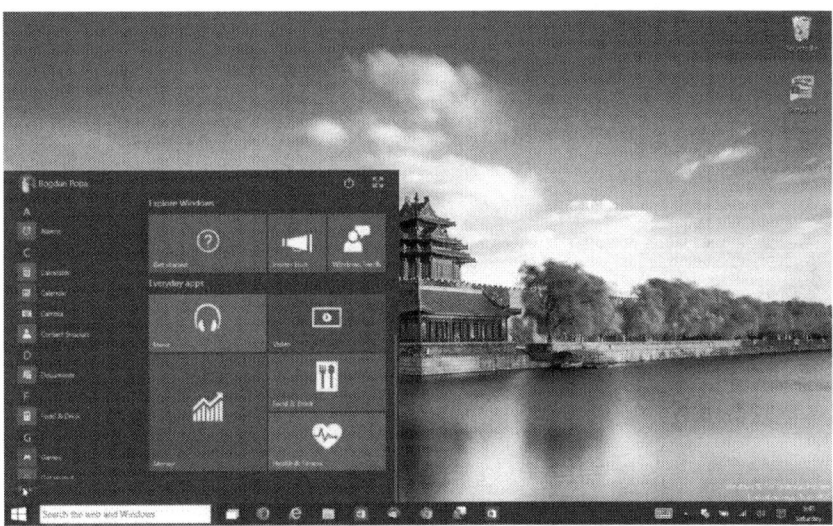

There are two main sections to the app, Collections and Albums. The Collections section will display a collection of all photos, grouped by date taken, oldest first. If users want to find a photo from a particular time period and not scroll through the library, click/tap on the date to zoom out to see all possible month choices available.

The Albums section is where the app intuitively creates photo albums for the user based on date taken and location. Initially only pictures in the Photos app will be from the Pictures folder and anything that is saved on OneDrive. Additional folders can be added to Photos through the *Settings* Menu, under the *Sources* section, by tapping/clicking *Add the folder to Pictures.*

The new editing features in the Photos app include filters, one-click enhance, and some basic fixes. Editing a photo within the Photos app is easy! Click on the photo and click on the pencil icon, which will open the editing options. The categories are well rounded with basic filters, fixes, effects, light, and color. Basic fixes are varied and include straightening, rotation, cropping, retouch, and red-eye elimination.

Brightness, highlights, shadows, and contrast can be adjusted in the Light Menu. Highlight and shadow adjustments work well with the features in the Color Menu to make pictures look their most vibrant. Filters and effects provide Instagram-like filters and lets users add things like tilt-shift to enhance composition.

You can always compare what you have edited with the original picture by clicking and holding the *Compare* button at the top of the screen. The top menu also contains the undo/redo buttons and all options to save or copy the original of the photo being edited.

The user can share pictures directly from the Photos app with the Windows 10 Share Toolbar. Share a single shot or an entire album by clicking select at the top of the screen and choosing individual photos and selecting the *Share* button that appears.

Pressing the Windows key and H will open the Share toolbar, and all the apps users can utilize to share photos such as, Facebook, Twitter, and Mail, will appear as your defaults.

Allow Photos to do the work and produce professional looking, edited media with just a couple taps and/or clicks. Put together an album of an entire summer vacation across Europe or make a special presentation to enhance a project at work or for the family. Photos archives, stores, and gets to know about the user's picture style all within the working screens of the application.

Chapter 4: Apps

The Apps integration and update is a big part of what makes Windows 10 so cool. There are now desktop apps that message, draw, edit, write, map, remember, note-take, call, order, and organize life for the user!

Here are some apps that are part of Windows 10 and others that are available through the Windows Store:

Maps

Maps is a universal app that looks good on all screen sizes. Combined features from Bing Maps and HERE Maps means the app is comfortable in its appearance and functionality. Add location pins to the start menu and share locations with friends in Mail or OneNote. Real-time traffic information is also provided along with search results, navigation, and public transit options. Satellite and street views are both available.

Groove Music

Windows 10 has a name for their Microsoft music app: Groove Music. Make playlists, listen to new music, or sing along with favorites. Customizable radio stations based on the user's most popular music picks makes listening to the radio all afternoon an easy experience. Groove Music Pass also provides upgraded, ad-free access to the music stations you love.

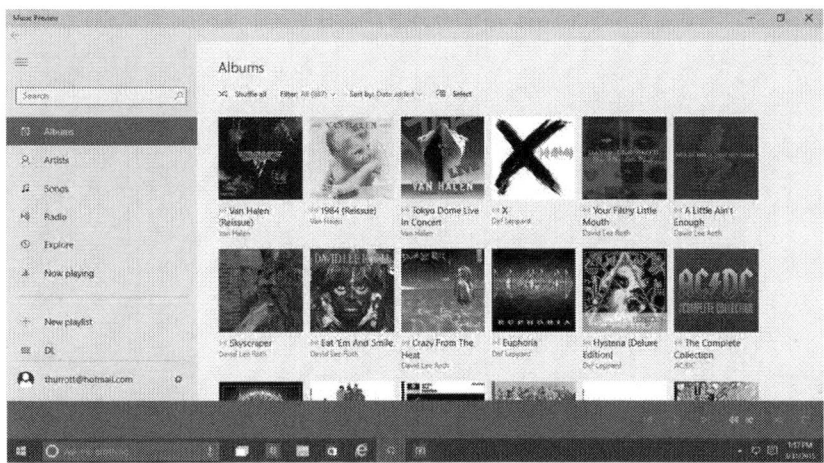

Movies & TV

With this 'double' app users can browse videos that they own or rent through streaming services online. Play content back with a keyboard, touch, or mouse and access the Windows Store to rent or purchase media. The Windows Store is intuitive and will suggest content for the user to peruse, view, or purchase. Movies & TV will also import your entire video collection and play it back, syncing functions between all devices so that no moment is ever missed!

Mail

Built-in Mail is fully integrated with Microsoft Word and Office, allowing the easy insertion of tables, bullets, pictures, and color in the user's email authoring process. The app also supports innovative touch gestures on tablets to assist in sorting, archiving, and reading mail. The updated navigation bar means that the user can now move freely between a calendar and emails, improving efficiency and productivity!

Calendar

The Calendar app lets users organize their appointments, view their week's or month's schedule, manage multiple calendar accounts, and set up reminders for tasks and emails.

Fun Third-party Apps:

Wunderlist (Windows store)

Use it to develop projects, plan trips, make lists, and store ideas. Wunderlist also allows collaboration and the sharing of lists with others. Fully integrated, Wunderlist will make the user's stuff accessible on any device, phone, tablet, or PC.

Plex (Windows store)

Check out phone or tablet videos on a PC. Stream any media, one device to another and back again. As a cross-platform app, Plex assists in quick access to multiple files on different devices.

Skitch

An excellent application for collaborating at the office or detailing how to get all the animals to their vet and groomer on the same day with the fewest trips. Skitch also shares screenshots and allows annotations with text, drawings, and arrows.

Nextgen Reader

For the news junkie! Nextgen Reader is the most comprehensive application for news that users will find with Windows 10. At a $1.99 purchase price, the app is affordable, and provides a clean, synced experience that works well with tablet or PC input interfaces. Users may sync for offline support, pin feeds to the Start Menu for news updates and trending stories, and much, much more.

Steam

Steam is the downloadable storefront of Valve. The PC user can purchase popular games, independent titles, and everything else. Users can connect the PC up to a TV and use the Big Picture Mode to manage and access the PC as a gaming, viewing, or interactive console.

Drawboard

Wonderful for marking up PDFs, Drawboard PDF has an easy to understand interface and many useful tools. Perfect for the architect or designer, Drawboard is solid with a stylus and allows the user to add manual annotations to PDF documents. Leave the briefcase at home, no need for paper here!

Universal and third-party applications will add a level of functionality to Windows 10 that has, as of yet, been elusive between platforms running Microsoft operating systems. Work and personal tasks can be timed, managed, documented, shared, and commented on. Mail and Word work together to simplify and homogenize the tasks within emailing, allowing the user to work between text, tables, and data, inserting all into an email without critical and detrimental losses of information integrity and formatting.

Chapter 5: Quick Guide

Before jumping in to install Windows 10, prepare the computer to ensure the upgrade process is seamless. Here is the process for checking updates, creating a system image, and backing up personal, user information prior to Windows 10 installation.

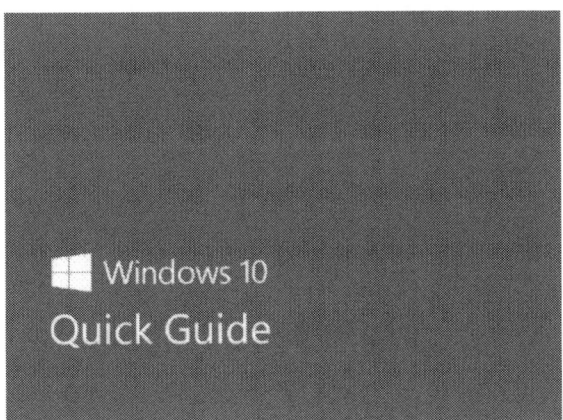

Windows 10 has the same minimum hardware requirements as Windows 7:

- Processor Speed: 1GHz CPU or faster
- RAM: 1GB (32-bit) or 2GB (64-bit)
- Disk space (c:): 16GB (32-bit) or 20GB (64-bit)

- Graphics Pack: DirectX 9-capable video card with WDDM driver

Check to see if the machine is able to run Windows 10 directly off the desktop. The process will require a tablet or desktop running Windows 7 Service Pack 1 or the Windows 8.1 update.

From the desktop, click on the small Windows icon located at the right-end of the taskbar, and select the *Check my PC* option from the left menu.

Free up space

Windows 10 Upgrade requires 16GB of available space to process. To assess the amount of free space on the hard drive open *Computer* and right-click on the *C:/ drive* and select *Properties*. Space can be liberated by selecting *Disk Cleanup*. If there are unused programs on the machine it is also recommended that they are uninstalled to free up additional hard drive space. In Windows 8, programs can be uninstalled easily through the *Control Panel*.

Back up all data to the cloud or an external drive

Backing up data is always a good idea. Cloud services like OneDrive, DropBox, or Google Drive, are great for data accessibility from anywhere. You can also use an external hard drive, which provides mass storage in private quarters. Just drag and drop personal files such as music, photos, and videos that the user would like to keep safe.

Windows 8 users can also use the *File History* feature to automatically back up personal files.

Create a system image

Windows 7 and Windows 8.1 both come with a tool that enables creation of a system image, which is a full backup of everything on the computer. From the *Control Panel* choose *Back up your computer* in the *Systems and Security* section. On the left, select create a system image and pick the location to save it in. An external drive is best. Then click *Next*, confirm that everything appears correct, and click *Start Backup*. When the process has finished, the user will have the option to create a system repair disc. This can be used to help with repairs to Windows if there are problems.

To restore the PC from a system image, go to the *Control Panel*. Begin by typing 'recovery' in the search box, click *Recovery* > select the system image that was created earlier.

Update device drivers

When installing a new version of Windows, it's always a good idea to check for compatible drivers.

Having the most updated drivers will solve most of the stability issues that could arise because of your computer's hardware.

To check for drivers, head to the specific PC manufacturer's support website. Downloading the drivers to an external thumb drive is helpful in case they are required during the installation process.

Now that the computer is backed up and optimized it is time to upgrade the operating system to Windows 10.

Step 1: Check Eligibility for Windows 10

1. Windows 10 is free for anyone running the latest version of Windows 7, Windows 8, and Windows 8.1 on their laptop, desktop, or tablet computer.
2. Users can figure out which version is on the computer by heading to Microsoft's website.
3. Users must be an administrator on the computer, meaning that the user owns the computer and has set it up personally. It's very likely that most users will not be able to update work computers that are managed by an IT department without their guidance.

Step 2: Back up your computer

To protect all of the files, back up the computer prior to upgrading the operating system.

Step 3: Update your current Windows version

All of the updates for the current version of Windows must be installed prior to the operating system upgrade. If a user has set up automatic updates that should do it, but double check first to be certain.

1. In Windows 7, go to *Start* > *Control Panel* > *System and Security* > *Windows Update*.
2. In Windows 8 and 8.1, go to *Start* > *PC Settings* > *Update and Recovery* > *Windows Update*.
3. The computer will alert the user if there are any available updates and walk users through the process of downloading and installing them.
4. Updates may need to be installed several times to finish the process.

Step 4: Wait for the Windows 10 prompt

Once the computer has all updates, users will need to wait patiently for a Windows icon to display in the taskbar on the desktop. Follow the directions on the screen to let Microsoft know that the user would like the Windows 10 update. Users can enter an email address to confirm the update, but it is not required.

Microsoft will then automatically send Windows 10 to the computer. The process can take several days or weeks. Users will be notified by the computer when the Windows 10 update files have been received.

Chapter 6: Tips & Tricks

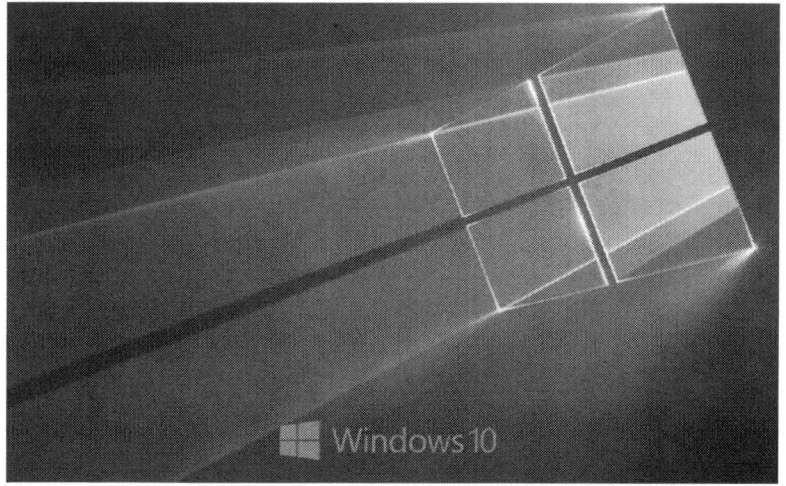

Here are some helpful tips and tricks for Windows 10. Included are: turning off Wi-Fi Sense, changing the platform's appearance, and customizable menus. There are always new tricks, so enjoy these and look for more coming soon!

Change the taskbar color

1. Right-click the desktop and choose *Personalize*.
2. Select *Colors*.
3. Choose a color; this will change the color for both the taskbar and start menu.
4. Want the highlights to match the backdrop? Turn on the *Automatically pick an accent color* option.

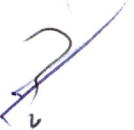

Select Default browser

1. Click the *Start* button.
2. Click *Settings*.
3. Click *System*.
4. Click *Default Apps*.
5. Scroll down and select *Web Browser*.
6. Choose your desired web browser.

Enable 'Hey Cortana'

1. Click within the search field on the taskbar
2. Click *Notebook*.
3. Click *Settings*.
4. Turn on *Hey Cortana*.
5. Optional: Click the *Learn my Voice* button so that Cortana familiarizes with the specific user's voice.

Manage Your Privacy Settings

1. Click the *Start* button.
2. Click *Settings*.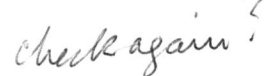
3. Click *Privacy*.
4. Privacy is divided into 13 sections. Disable anything that may look intrusive.

Turn on Battery Saver

1. Click the *Start* button.
2. Click *Settings*.
3. Click *System*.
4. Click *Battery Saver*.

Turn on the Start Screen

1. Right-click the desktop and choose *Personalize*.
2. Select *Start*.
3. Turn on *Use Start full screen*.

Add folders to the Start Menu

1. Right-click the desktop and choose *Personalize*.
2. Select *Start*.
3. Click *Choose which folders appear on Start*.

Remove tiles from Start Menu

1. Click the *Start* button.
2. Right-click the tile to be removed.
3. Choose *Unpin from Start*.

Change Notification Behavior

1. Click the *Start* button.
2. Click *Settings*.
3. Click *System*.
4. Click *Notifications & Actions*.
5. Choose a desired setting for notifications.

Turn on Inactive Page Scrolling

1. Click *Start* button.
2. Click *Settings*.
3. Click *Devices*.
4. Select *Mouse & Touchpad*.
5. Make sure *Scroll inactive windows when I hover over them* is checked.

Clear Cortana's Information Stash

1. Login to https://www.bing.com/account/personalization
2. This is where users clear Cortana data such as personalized speech, search history, interests, saved places, other Cortana data, inking, and typing.

Disable automatic restarts

1. Click the *Start* button.
2. Click *Settings*.
3. Click *Update & Security*.
4. Click *Windows update*.
5. Click *Advanced Options*.
6. Choose *Notify to schedule restart* from the dropdown menu.

Create GodMode Tool

1. Right-click the desktop.
2. Click *New*.
3. Click *Folder*.
4. Rename folder to this: *GodMode.{ED7BA470-8E54-465E-825C-99712043E01C}*
5. The user should now have an icon labeled GodMode.

Disable Wi-Fi Sharing

1. Click the *Start* button.
2. Click *Settings*.
3. Click *Network & Internet*.
4. Scroll down and click *Manage Wi-Fi Settings*.
5. Uncheck everything listed under *For networks I select, share them with my*....

Uninstall a Program

1. Right-click the *Start* button.
2. Click *Programs & Features*.
3. Choose the program to uninstall.

Keep Cortana from Sending Your Browser History to Microsoft

1. Open the Edge browser.
2. Click the button with three dots.
3. Choose *Settings*.
4. Choose *View Advanced Settings*.
5. Turn off *Have Cortana Assist Me in Microsoft Edge*.
6. Turn off *Use page prediction to speed up browsing, improve reading, and make my overall experience better*.

Change Default Search Engine in Edge

1. Open the Edge browser.
2. Click the button with three dots.
3. Choose *Settings*.
4. Choose *View Advanced Settings*.
5. Choose a search engine in the '*Search in the address bar with* dropdown menu.

- *Print to PDF*

With Windows 10 you can now save and subsequently print documents as PDF without using a third-party program. In previous editions of Windows you could only Export to PDF. This is a feature that's been a long time coming.

- *Use Maps Offline*

Most likely updated or installed with your Windows 10 update, the new Microsoft Maps lets you work offline. To download or update maps open *Start* > Choose *Settings* > *System* > Choose *Download Maps*.

You can also allow Windows to automatically search for any Maps updates. To do this open *Start* > Choose *Settings* > *System* > Toggle *Automatically Update Maps* to On.

Keyboard Shortcuts

-To Open:

Open Action Center	Windows Logo Key + A
Open an app	Shift + Click a taskbar icon
Open an app as an administrator	Ctrl + Shift + Click a taskbar icon
Open Cortana – to listen to a	Windows Logo Key + C

command	
Open Ease of Access Centre	Windows Logo Key + U
Open File Explorer	Windows Logo Key + E
Open Narrator	Windows Logo Key + Enter
Open Settings	Windows Logo Key + I
Open Search	Windows Logo Key + S
Open Share Charm	Windows Logo Key + H
Open Start	Ctrl + Esc
Open the shortcut menu for the active window	Alt + Spacebar
Open Task Manager	Ctrl + Shift + Esc
Open Task View	Windows Logo Key + Tab
Open the Run dialogue box	Windows Logo Key + R

Open the Quick Link menu	Windows Logo Key + X

- *General Shortcuts*

Switch between open apps	Alt + Tab
Display properties for selected item	Alt + Enter
Open the shortcut menu for the active window	Alt + Spacebar
Close the open app	Alt + F4
Go forward	Alt + Right Arrow
Go back	Alt + Left arrow
Rename the selected item	F2
Search for a file or folder in File Explorer	F3
Display the address bar list in File Explorer	F4
Refresh the active window	F5

Cycle though screen elements in a window or on the desktop	F6
Activate the menu bar in the active app	F10
Select all items in a document or window	Ctrl + A
Delete the selected item	Ctrl + D or Delete
Copy selected item	Ctrl + C
Refresh the active window	Ctrl + R or F5
Paste selected item	Ctrl + V
Cut selected item	Ctrl + X
Undo an action	Ctrl + Z
Redo an action	Ctrl + Y
Select a block of text	Ctrl + Shift with an array key
Minimize all windows	Windows Logo Key + M
Display and hide desktop	Windows Logo Key + D
Lock your PC or switch accounts	Windows Logo Key + L
Lock device orientation	Windows Logo Key + O

Temporarily switch to the desktop	Windows Logo Key + comma
Add a virtual desktop	Windows Logo Key + Ctrl + D
Switch between virtual desktops you've created on the right	Windows Logo Key + Ctrl + Right
Switch between virtual desktops you've created on the left	Windows Logp Key + Ctrl + Left

New tips and tricks will constantly be updated for Windows 10. Check for available unique tips for third-party applications, too. As new applications are made available for the operating system, tricks to enhance their functionality should be readily accessible through a verbal search in Edge with Cortana's help.

Play XBOX games on your PC

Another much heralded and fun new function is the ability to play Xbox One games on your Windows PC! Using the connected game streaming function, you can play the games you have on your Xbox One on your PC as well, even using a controller if you have one.

The feature isn't perfect and because it's a stream, there are slight lags. This means playing Multiplayer games can be uncomfortable, but for anything else, it's a great feature!

Chapter 7: How To Repair Common Problems

No matter which operating system you use there is always a small chance that you could encounter some software problems. These can be triggered by a number of factors including system updates and the installation of new hardware. In this chapter we will guide you through ways in which you can resolve these issues. Sometimes you will need to create installation media or restore your PC to an earlier restore point.

Recover and Restore

If the problem you are encountering with your PC means that you cannot open the *Settings Menu* you can restart your PC from the sign-in screen.

To open the sign-in screen if you have already logged in: press the Windows Key on your keyboard and L.

Once the log-in screen has loaded, you can restart your PC. To do this: hold the *Shift* key on your keyboard > Select the *Power* icon > Choose *Restart*.

Once your PC has begun to restart select *Troubleshoot* from the menu prompt > Choose *Reset This PC*.

-*To Create Installation Media*

Visit http://go.microsoft.com/fwlink/p/?LinkID=616447 on a working PC > Download the media creation tool > Then *Run* the download. This will open a wizard. Select your choices for the language, edition, and architecture > Follow the rest of the wizard to create the installation media, selecting the required fields and pressing *Next*. Once you have completed the wizard select *Finish*.

Your installation media has now been created.

-*To Restore from System Restore Point*

Why would you need this?

You would use this function if your PC isn't working well and you have recently installed an update, app, or new driver.

Using this process to restore your PC will return it to an early point in time. This is called a restore point. Restore points are automatically created by Windows when you install updates, apps, drivers, and when you manually create them.

-How to restore from system restore points.

Begin by launching the *Start Menu* > Choose *Settings* > Select *Update and Security* > Choose *Recovery* from the left-hand side navigation panel > Click *Get Started* underneath *Reset this PC*.

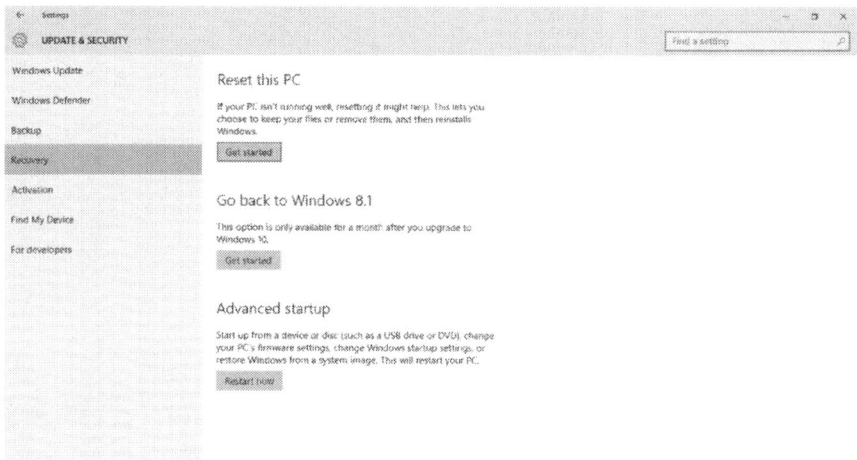

Next, choose *Keep My Files* from the *Choose an option* pop up.

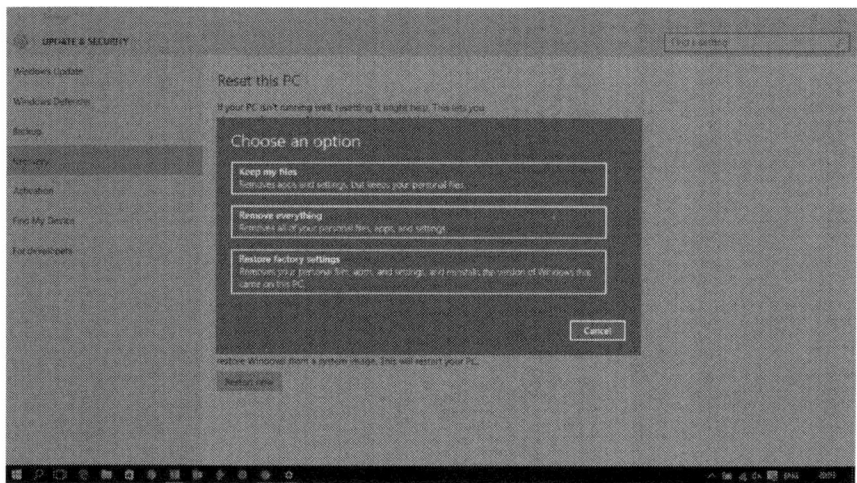

Now follow the instructions prompted by the wizard. Once the wizard has finished, your PC will restart from your chosen restore point.

-To Reset your PC

Why would you want to reset your PC?

If you have been experiencing problems with your PC but you haven't installed an update, app, or new driver recently it may help to reset your PC.

Note that by resetting your PC you will remove all data that is stored on your PC. It is therefore advised that you create an external backup of the data you wish to keep.

How to reset your PC.

Begin by pressing the *Start* icon to launch the *Start Menu* > Choose *Settings* > Select *Update and Security* > Choose *Recovery* from the left-hand side navigation panel > Click *Get Started* underneath *Reset*.

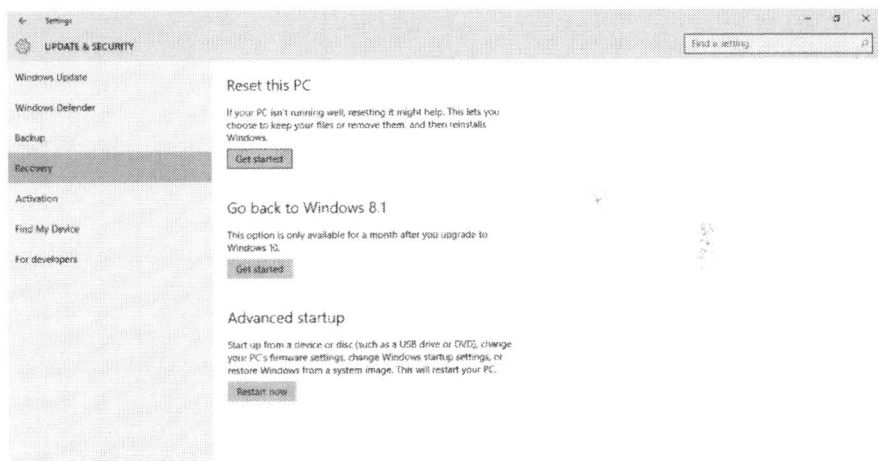

Next, choose *Remove Everything* from the *Choose an option* pop up. You can also choose *Restore to factory settings* but note that this will return your PC to the original operating system as well as wiping all data stored on your PC.

-*To Restore or Reset your PC using a Recovery Drive*

Why would you need to restore or reset your PC using a recovery drive?

If you have previously created a recovery drive you can use this option to restore or reset your PC if it isn't working properly.

If you are using a recovery drive which you created on Windows 10:

Ensure your PC is switched off > Connect the recovery drive to your PC > Turn your PC on > When the *Choose an option* screen pops up select *Troubleshoot* > Follow the wizard prompts.

If *Choose an option* window does not launch when you turn your PC on, first try re-connecting your recovery drive. If the *Choose an option* window still does not launch, check with your PC's manufacturer about the various ways in which you can change your PC's boot order.

If you are using a recovery drive created on Windows 8.1

Ensure your PC is switched off > Connect the recovery drive you have created > Turn your PC on.

When the *Choose an option* screen pops up select *Troubleshoot*. This will provide you with two options:

To Restore: Select *Advanced Settings* > Choose *System Restore*.

To Reset: Select *Reset this PC*

Again, if the *Choose an Option* menu does not launch when you turn your PC on, try re-connecting your recovery drive. If the *Choose an option* window still does not launch, check with your PC's manufacturer about the various ways in which you can change your PC's boot order.

-*To Restore or Reset your PC using installation media*

Why would you need to use installation media to restore or reset your PC?

If you haven't created a recovery drive and your PC is not working properly you can create installation media to restore or reset your PC. In order to do this you will need the use of a fully working PC and you will need to create installation media.

If you need to create installation media:

Visit http://go.microsoft.com/fwlink/p/?LinkID=616447 on a working PC > Download the media creation tool > Run the downloaded file > Follow the pop-up wizard and select your chosen language, edition, and architecture from the dropdown fields > Press *Next* > Once completed, select *Finish*.

Once you have created your installation media:

Connect the installation media to the PC that is not fully working > Turn the PC on > Enter your language and preferences from the start up screen > Select *Next* > Select *Repair your computer* > On the *Choose an option* window select *Troubleshoot* > This gives you two options:

1) To Restore: Select *Advanced Settings* > Choose *System Restore*.

or

2) To Reset: Select *Reset this PC*

-*System Error Codes*

Microsoft has designed each of its system error codes to cover a large range of problems. These codes have been designed with the intention that they will be used by programmers and therefore require a lot of in-depth knowledge to investigate, analyze, and correct. If you have identified that your PC is displaying a system error code, make sure to note down the exact configuration of the code, including any brackets.

Once you have taken note of the code, visit: http://support.microsoft.com and log your problem with the support team and await a response.

Screen Problems

-*Screen Flickering*

If you are experiencing a flickering screen in Windows 10 you can determine what is causing this problem by visiting the *Task Manager*. To do this:

Press the *Ctrl+Shift+Esc* keys at the same time or launch the *Start Menu* > Choose *Task Manager*. [See below for an image of the Task Manager.]

WINDOWS 10

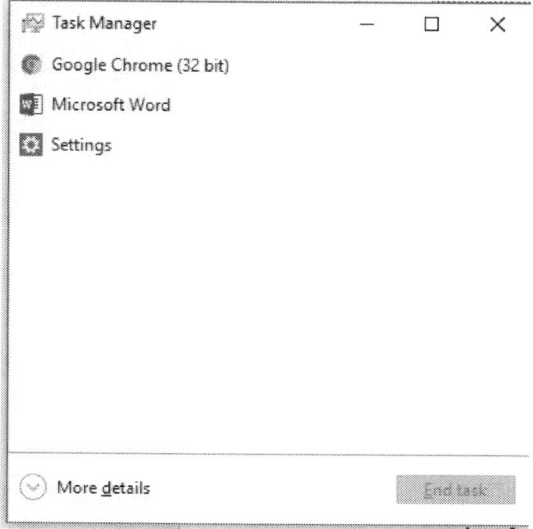

Once the Task Manager has opened you can determine what issue you are experiencing. To do this you will need to inspect whether the Task Manager window is flickering or not.

If the Task Manager flickers you can determine that a **display driver** is the probable cause of the problem. But, if the Task Manager does not appear to flicker then **an app** is most likely causing the problem.

To resolve an issue that is caused by a display driver you will need to update your display driver. To do this: start your PC in *Safe Mode*. You can do this from *Settings* or from the *Sign-in Screen*. From *Settings*, launch the *Start Menu* > Choose *Settings* > Select *Update and Security* > Choose *Recovery* from the left-hand navigation panel > Underneath the heading *Advanced Start Up*, select *Restart Now*.

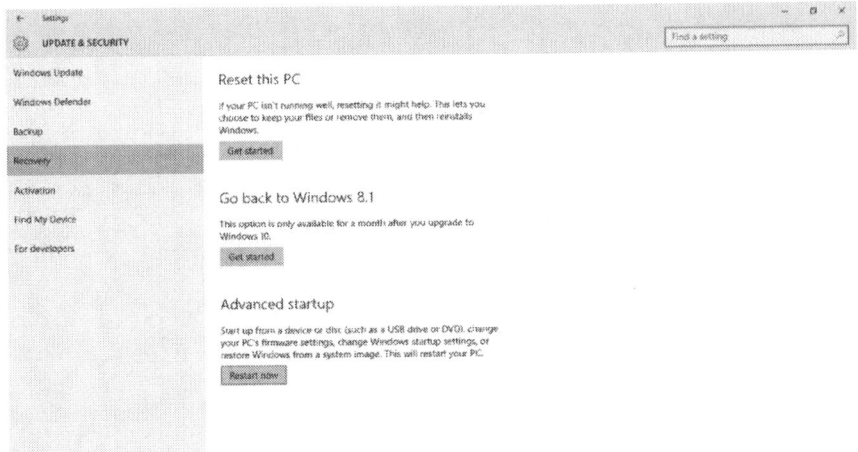

Next, wait for your PC to restart. The *Choose an Option* screen will launch > Select *Troubleshoot* > Select *Advanced Options* > Select *Startup Settings* > Choose *Restart*. Once your PC starts, a list of options will be displayed > Select 4 or F4 to start your PC in *Safe Mode*, or if you need to use the Internet select 5 or F5 to start your PC in *Safe Mode with Networking*.

Once you have started your PC in Safe Mode follow these steps:

Right-click on the *Start* button > Select *Device Manager* from the list.

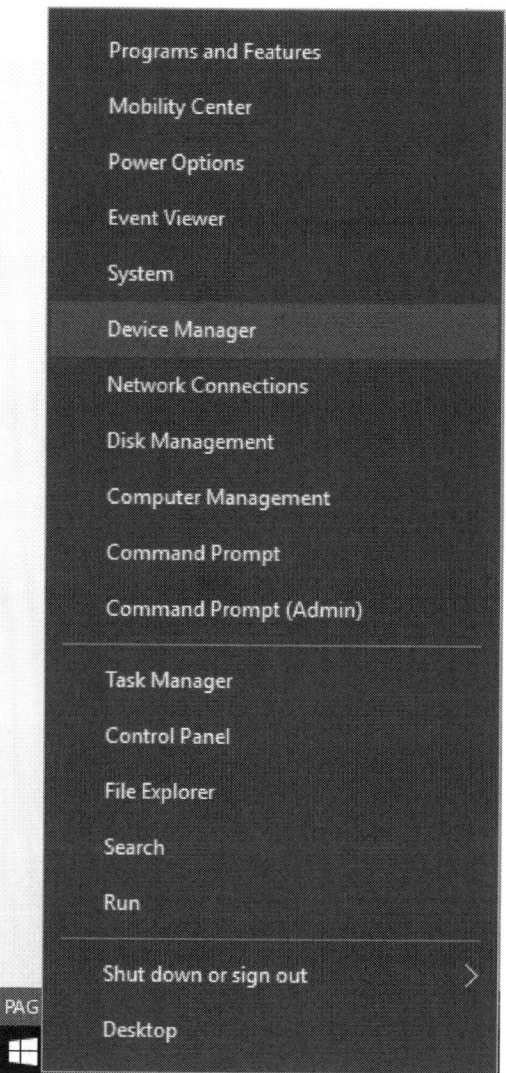

Expand the *Display adapters* section by clicking on the expand arrow.

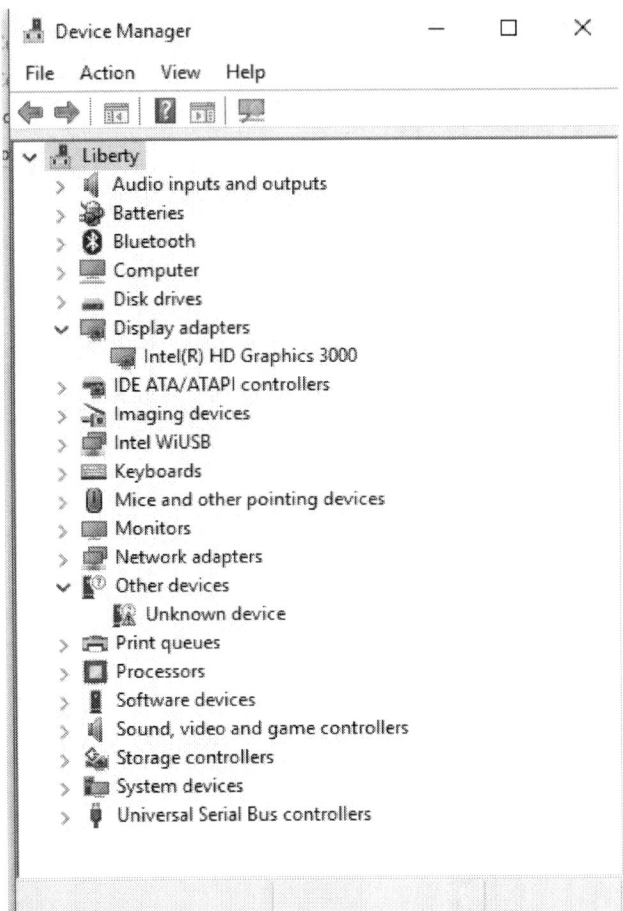

Right-click the listed adapter > Select *Uninstall.*

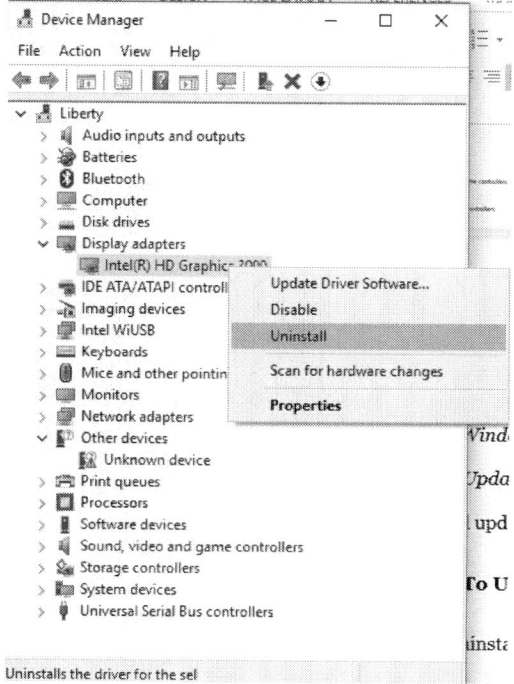

In the pop-up window ensure the checkbox *Delete the driver software for this device* is ticked and select *OK*.

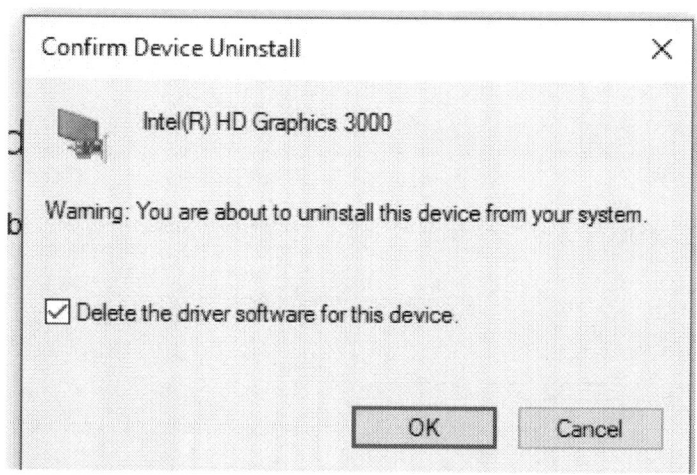

Restart your PC.

Once your PC restarts, open the *Settings Menu* > Select *Update and Security* > Choose *Windows Update* from the left-hand side navigation panel > Click *Check for Updates*.

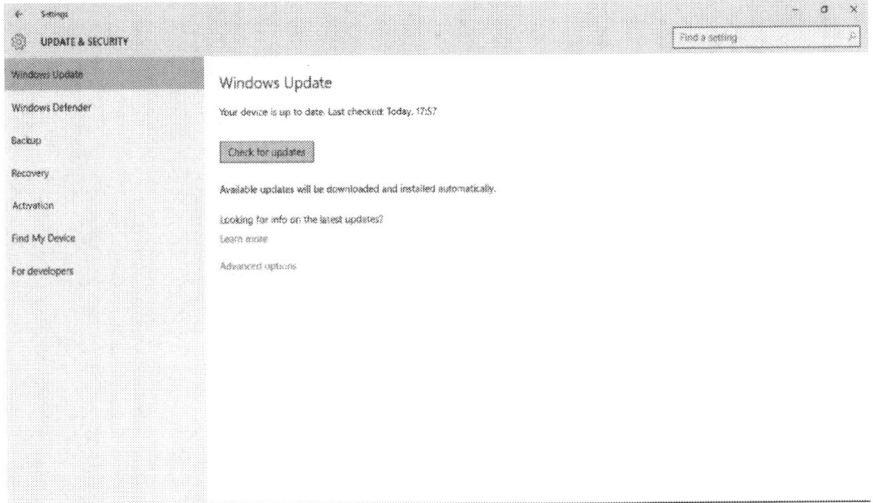

This should find the update to your device driver. Follow the wizard and update the device driver.

To resolve screen flickering that has been caused by the recent installation of an app you will need to uninstall the required app. You can do these from either the *Start* or *Settings* menu.

To uninstall from the Start Menu, launch the *Start Menu* > Click *All Apps* > From the scrolling list find the app that you want to uninstall > Right-click on the app name > Choose *Uninstall* from the dropdown list.

WINDOWS 10

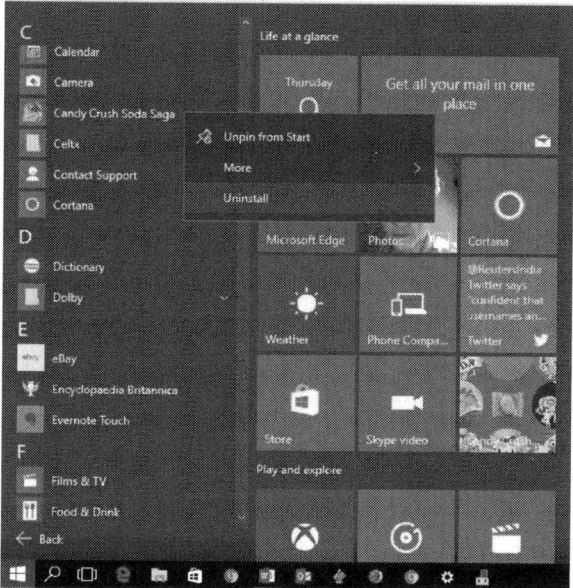

Windows may ask you to confirm your action in a *User Access Control Window* > Click *Yes*.

To uninstall from the Settings Menu > Launch the *Start Menu* > Choose *Settings* > Select *System*.

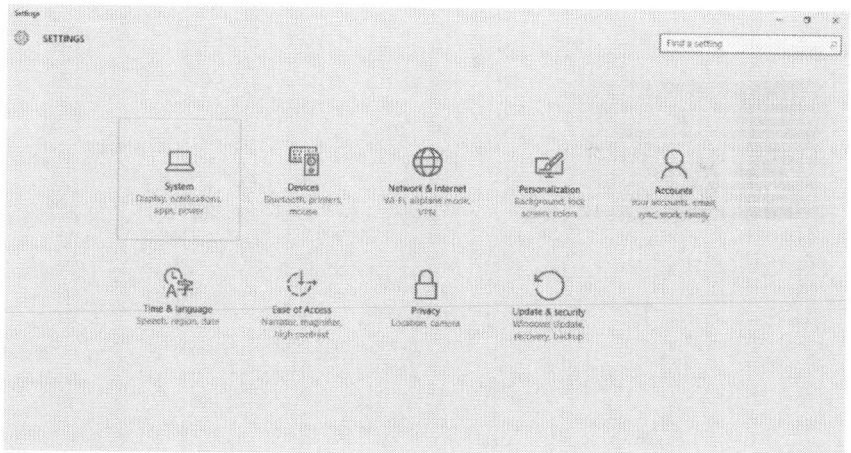

Choose *Apps & Features* > Scroll through the list of the apps and features and find the one that you want to uninstall > Click on the app name > Choose *Uninstall*.

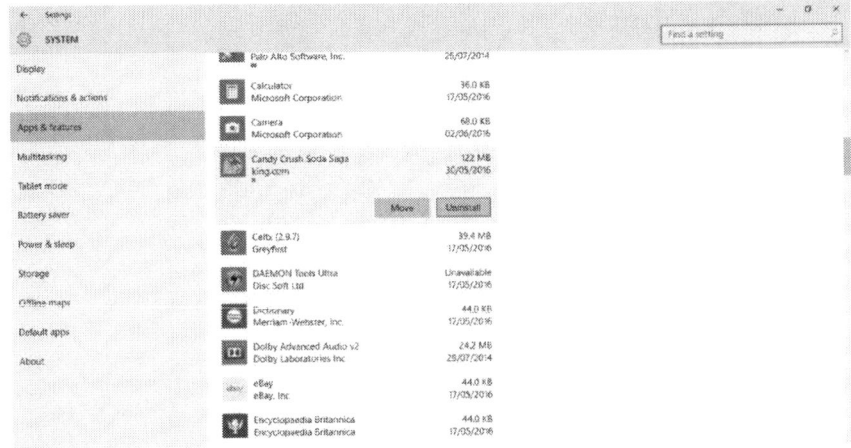

Windows may ask you to confirm your action in a *User Access Control Window* > Select *Yes* or *Uninstall*.

-*Black Screen Error*

If your PC is displaying a plain black screen you should first check that there is not an external fault with the hardware. To do this, check that every connection cable, the power adapters, and the display adapters are all correctly plugged in.

Next, double check that each of the connecting cables and adapters work by using a second display output.

If all the external connections are correct and there is no fault, you will need to start your PC in safe mode. To do this you will need an installation media on a DVD or USB.

To create installation media:

Visit http://go.microsoft.com/fwlink/p/?LinkID=616447 on a working PC > Download the media creation tool > Run the media creation tool > Choose the language, edition, and architecture >

Follow the wizard to create the installation media by selecting the required fields > Once complete select *Finish*.

Once you have created installation media > Turn your PC off > Insert the installation media > Start your PC > Select *Repair your computer* from the options displayed on launch > From the *Choose an Option* screen select *Troubleshoot* > Select *Advanced Options* > Choose *Startup Settings* > *Restart*.

Once your PC has restarted, select 5 or press F5 to restart your PC in *Safe Mode with Networking*.

Once your PC has restarted in Safe Mode > Right-click on the *Start* icon > Choose *Device Manager* > Click on the arrow to expand the *Display Adapter*. This will display either one or two items.

If only one item is shown you will need to either *Rollback* the item or *uninstall* the display adapter. To do this: right-click on the display item > Select *Properties* > Choose *Driver* from the tabs > Choose either *Roll Back Driver* or *Uninstall* > Confirm this choice by selecting either *Yes* or *Okay*.

If two items are shown you will need to disable one of the display adapters. To do this: Restart your PC > Check if the error still exists > If the error has not been resolved restart your PC in safe mode > Open the device manager again by right clicking on the start icon and choosing *Device Manager* from the list > Enable the display adapter you previously disabled and disable the other item in the list > Restart your PC.

Once you have completed all the necessary steps shut down your PC > Disconnect the installation media > Turn your PC back on and check if the issue remains.

-Blue Screen Error

If your PC restarts or shuts down because an unexpected problem has occurred you might see a blue screen error. With this error you won't be able to access some aspects of the usual Windows interface.

If you experienced the blue screen error whilst using your PC you can try one of following options to try and resolve the issue.

1) Check for updates > In the search box on the taskbar type *Windows Update* > Select *Windows Update* to open the window > Choose *Check for Updates* > Follow any instructions if there is an update available.

2) Remove newly installed hardware > If you have recently added new hardware to your PC this could be the cause of your blue screen error. Remove the newly installed hardware by turning off your PC > Unplug > Restart your PC.

If you experienced the blue screen error after an update has been installed onto your PC you will need to uninstall the recent update to resolve the issue. The process to do this will depend on whether you can access the desktop or not.

If you can access the desktop > Type *View installed updates* into the search box on the taskbar.

WINDOWS 10

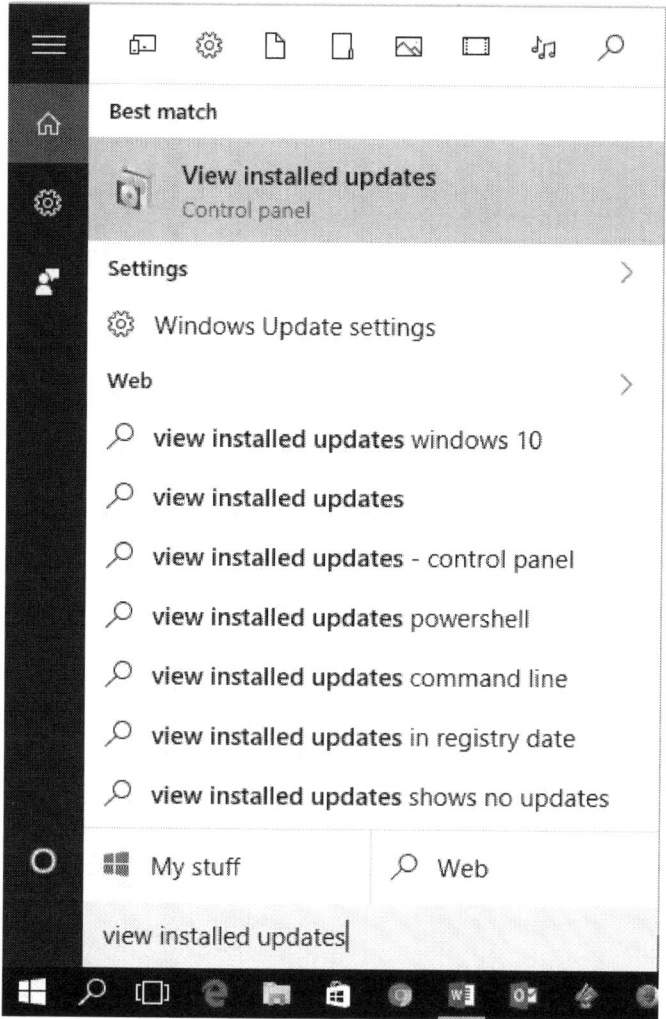

Choose *View installed updates* > Drag and expand the window so that you can see the install date and select the most recent update that you want to uninstall. You can also choose a specific date for installations. To do this, click the arrow on the tab *Installed on*.

Select *Uninstall* from the top bar.

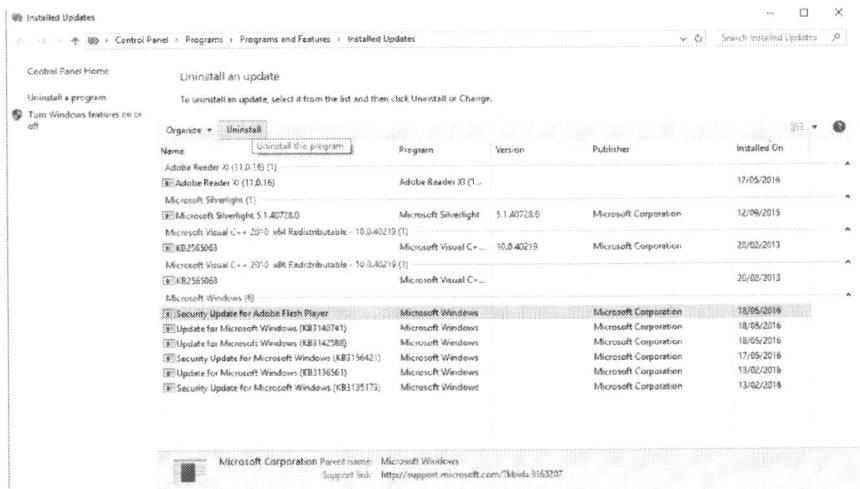

Restart your PC.

If you can't access the desktop you will enter into automatic repair after it has restarted several times. Once your PC is in the automatic repair mode select *Troubleshoot* from the *Choose an option* screen > Select *Advanced Options* > Choose *System Restore*. This will return your PC to a previous version of your PC using a restore point.

Note: If either of these methods resolves your blue screen issue you will want to temporarily block the update that caused this to occur from automatically installing again.

Chapter 8: Windows Update Delivery Optimization

-*What is Windows Update Delivery Optimization?*

New to Windows 10 is Windows Update Delivery Optimization (WUDO). This allows you to get Windows updates and Windows Store apps from sources other than Microsoft. In simple terms, Windows can now download updates and apps from PCs which have previously installed the same download.

Some benefits of Delivery Optimization are:

- The amount of bandwidth you need to keep all your PCs up to date will reduce if you use Delivery Optimization.

- If you have a slow internet connection Delivery Optimization could also help by allowing you to update and install apps faster than before.

Be aware that by enabling Delivery Optimization, you will send updates and apps from your PC to other PCs across your local network and the Internet. You can, of course, choose which PCs you wish to download from and which to send updates to and from.

You can set WUDO to only use PCs that are on your local network. This means that part of the download will come from local PCs. But Windows will always refer to Microsoft for part of the download ensuring that the entire 100% of the download does not come from local PCs.

You can set WUDO to use both PCs on your local network and PCs on the Internet. This follows the same process as downloading updates and apps from PCs in your local network but also scans for PCs that are on the Internet which can provide part of the download.

Notably, Delivery Optimization cannot be used to download, send, access, or change ANY personal files or content.

Delivery Optimization will only send updates and apps to other PCs that you have downloaded through Windows Update or Windows Store. This is a feature that can be disabled.

-To Disable Delivery Optimization

Open the *Start Menu* > Choose *Settings* > Select *Update and Security*.

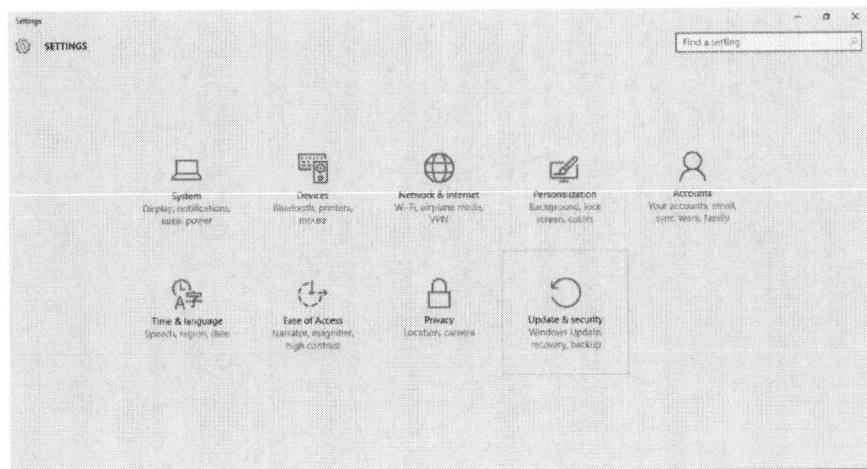

Choose *Windows Update* > Select *Advanced Options*.

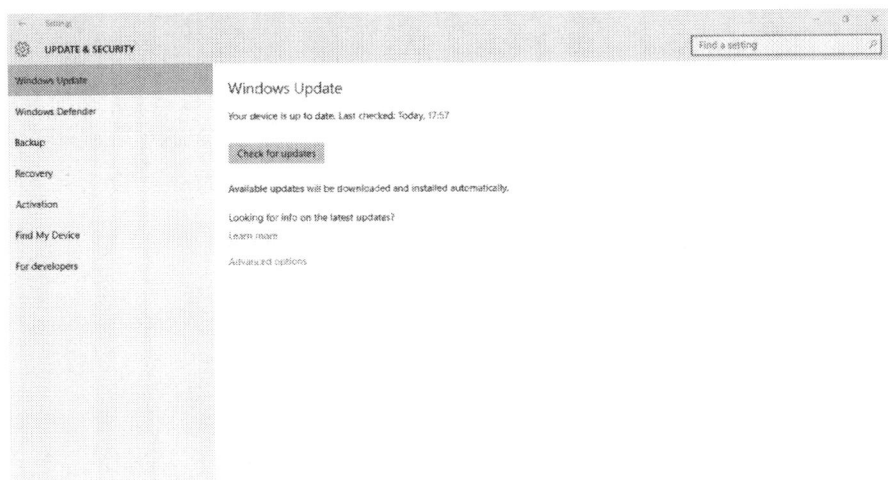

Select *Choose how updates are delivered*.

WINDOWS 10

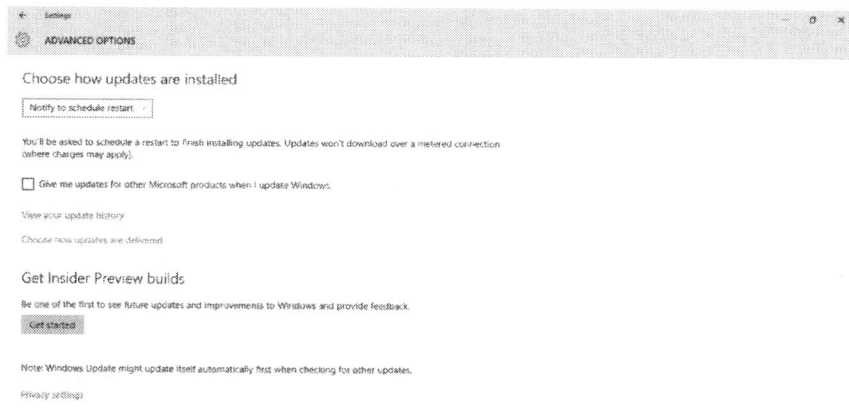

Toggle *Updates from more than one place* to *Off*.

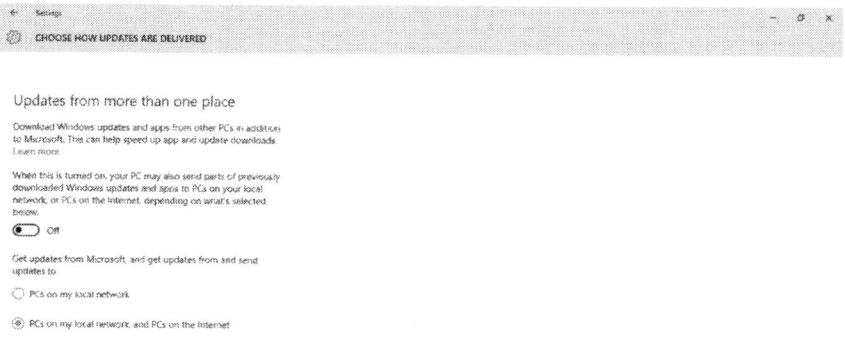

59

Chapter 9: Advanced Customizations

As you know, there are plenty of ways to personalize Windows 10. Here are some customizations that go beyond the taskbar, start menu, action center, and background image settings.

-Personalize The Lock Screen

With Windows 10 you can personalize your lock screen. To do this: open the *Settings Menu* > Choose *Personalization* > Select *Lock Screen* from the left-hand side navigation panel.

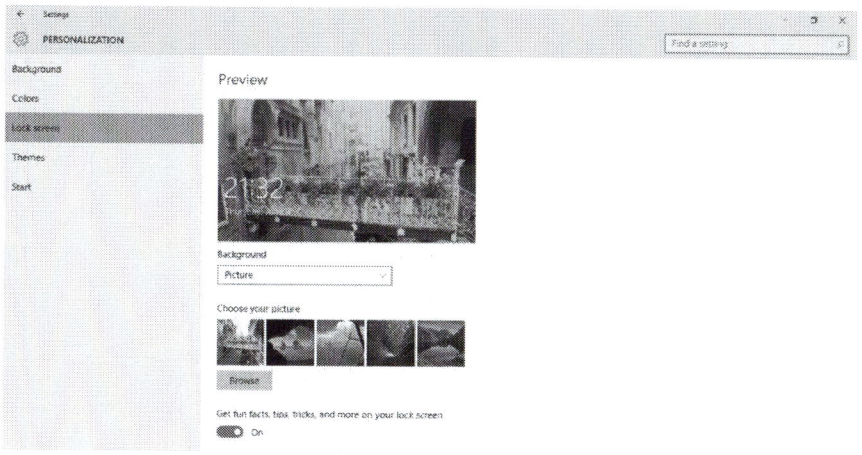

Here you can:

- Change your background picture from a range of pre-set wallpapers or from your picture library by clicking the *Browse* button.

- Decide whether to display fun facts and tips and tricks from displaying on the lock screen.

- Set the background to a slideshow. You can do this by clicking *Advanced Slideshow Settings*.

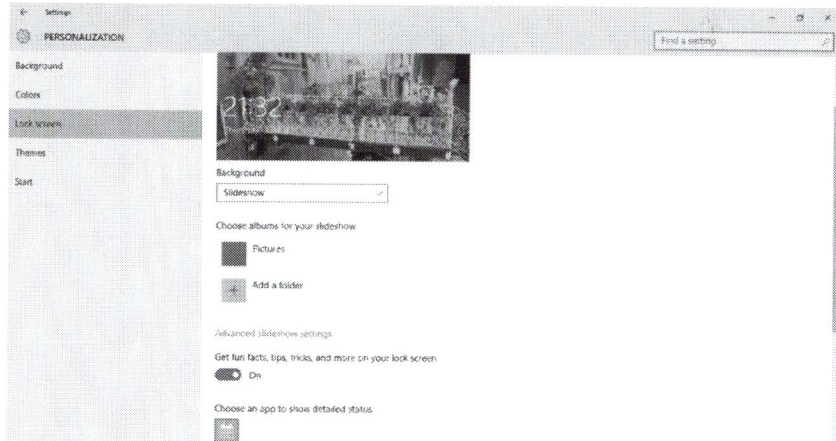

-Personalize Cortana

Cortana is your new digital assistant. Cortana is displayed at the bottom left of the taskbar. Cortana can help you find files, folders, apps, and more from your PC and also help you search the internet.

If you are in a country where the native language is different to your first language: open *Settings* > Choose *Time and Language* > Open *Speech* from the left-hand side navigation panel > Tick the checkbox *Recognize non-native accents for this language*.

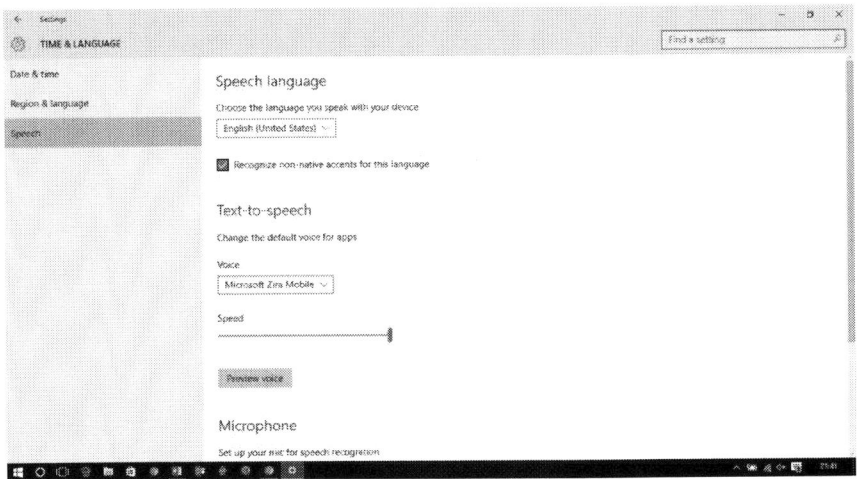

If you want to disable Cortana: open *Settings* > Select *Privacy* > Choose *Speech, inking and typing* from the left-hand panel > Click *Stop getting to know me*.

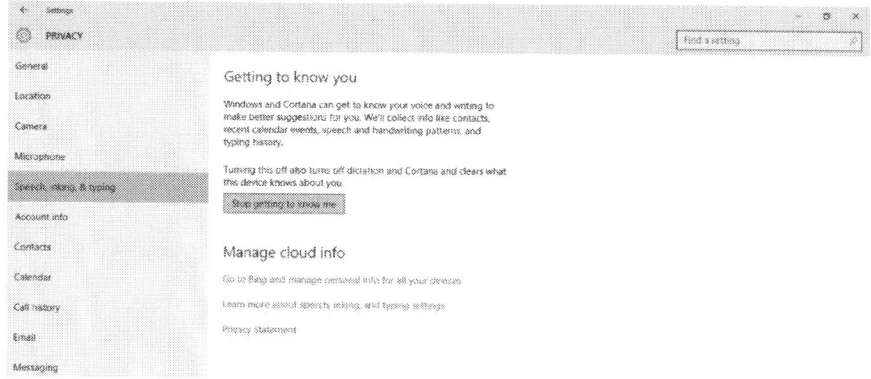

If you have decided to disable Cortana you may also want to delete any remaining data and personal information that Cortana has retained. To do this: open Cortana > Select the *Settings* icon from the left-hand side panel > Choose *Bing SafeSearch Settings*.

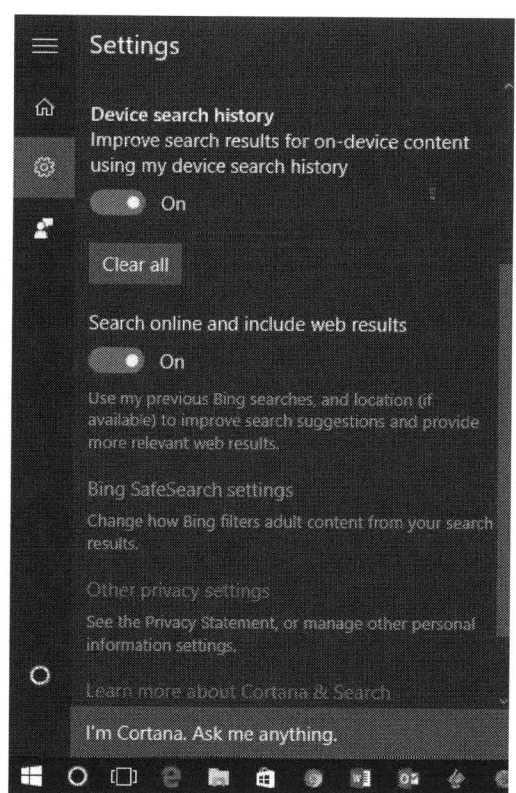

This will open a new window > Sign in to the account that you are using on your computer if you are asked to do so > Click the *Clear* button for *Clear Personal Info* and *Other Cortana Data and Personalized Speech, Inking and Typing* > Confirm deletion > Close Window

-Pin Apps and Files

Across the entire Windows 10 OS you can pin apps, contacts, documents, folders, and files. Starting with the start menu and taskbar and ranging to the folders such as documents, desktop, pictures, etc., this feature makes accessing what you want and need to be a quicker, smoother process.

-To Pin Apps to the Taskbar

Open the *Start Menu* > Choose *All Apps* > Access the jump list and click the desired letter *(to access the jump list click on any of the capitalized alphabetical letter headings)* > Find the desired application > Right-click > Choose *Pin to Taskbar* from the dropdown list. The application icon will then appear on the taskbar > Drag and drop the icon to move it across the taskbar.

-To Pin Files to Taskbar

Right-click on an application from the taskbar > This will bring up a list of recent documents or files below a section entitled *Pinned* > Hover over a recent document until the pin-like symbol appears on the right-hand side of the file name > Select this > The document or file will then appear in the *Pinned* section above.

-To Pin Files in Folders

Open *File Explorer* by using Cortana or the File Explorer Icon on the taskbar > Pin a folder or file by clicking on the *Pin* icon. This is shown on the right-hand side of folder names in the *Quick Access* navigation panel and underneath file locations in the *Frequent Folders* section.

-Send Microsoft Your Opinion

To send Microsoft feedback of your experience, whether that be negative, positive, or constructive, you can use the feedback app. This is alongside the occasional prompts Windows 10 will give you to provide feedback of its new operating system. To do this: open *Start Menu* > Select *All Apps* > Scroll through the list of apps until you find *Windows Feedback* (alternatively use the jump menu and select *W* then choose *Windows Feedback)*

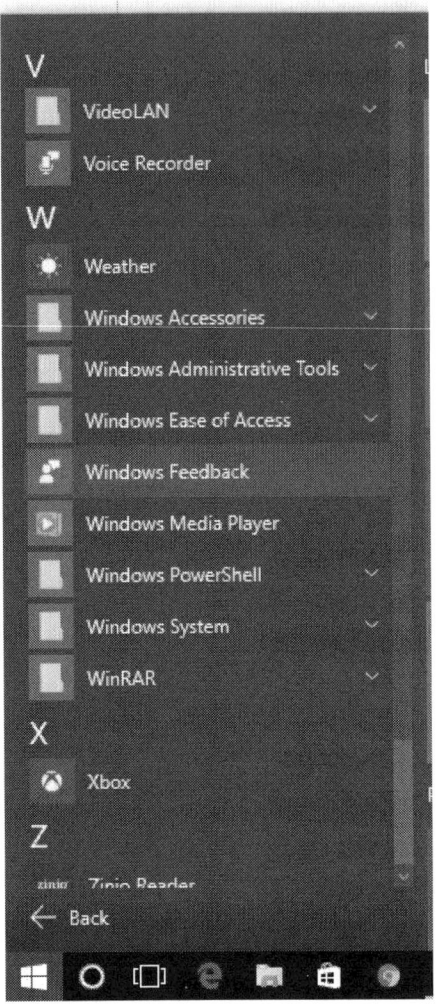

The first time you use Windows Feedback you will need to register for the *Windows Insider Program.* You can do this by logging in to your Microsoft Live account. But if you don't have one you will need to create an account to access this service. Click the link in the pop-up window.

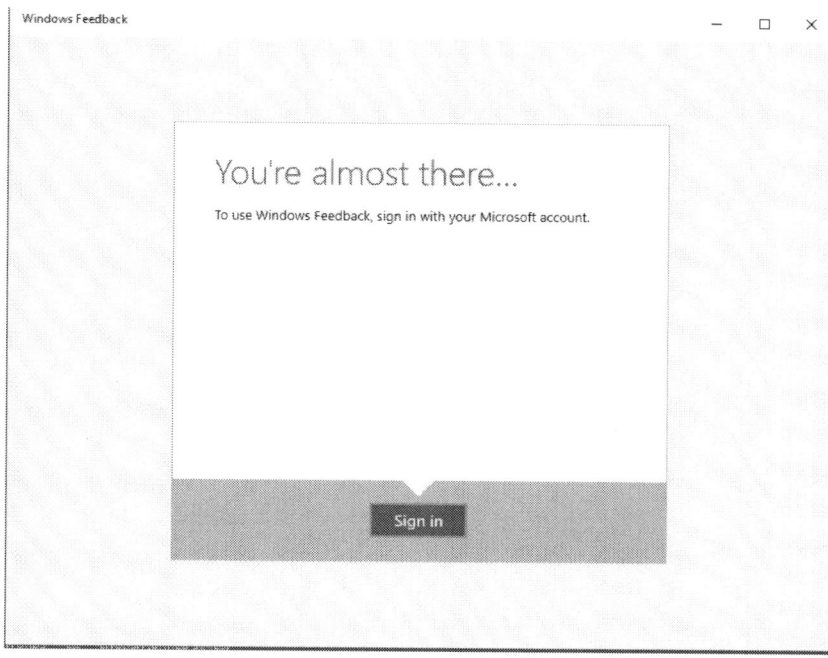

Once you have registered you can go back to the Windows Feedback app. The App will suggest areas for you to leave feedback in. This is based on your most recent and frequently used applications. You can also browse and look for a topic to leave feedback in by using the left-hand side navigation panel.

Before you choose to leave feedback on a topic it is worth searching the existing feedback to see if the issue has previously been logged. Use the *Search* option from the left-hand side navigation panel > Enter your search into the text box > If the option exists, select and add feedback to that thread. You can simply choose the option *Me Too* or *Add more details*.

If the topic you wish to log feedback for doesn't exist, click *New Feedback* underneath the *Search* option.

-Create Multiple Desktops

Another new feature to Windows 10 is the ability to create multiple desktops.

You can create a new desktop by following either of these steps:

1) Press the task view icon on the taskbar. This symbol resembles a rectangle with two small square brackets on either side.

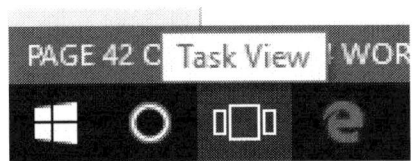

Once TaskView has loaded choose *New Desktop* from the right-hand side of the screen to create a new desktop.

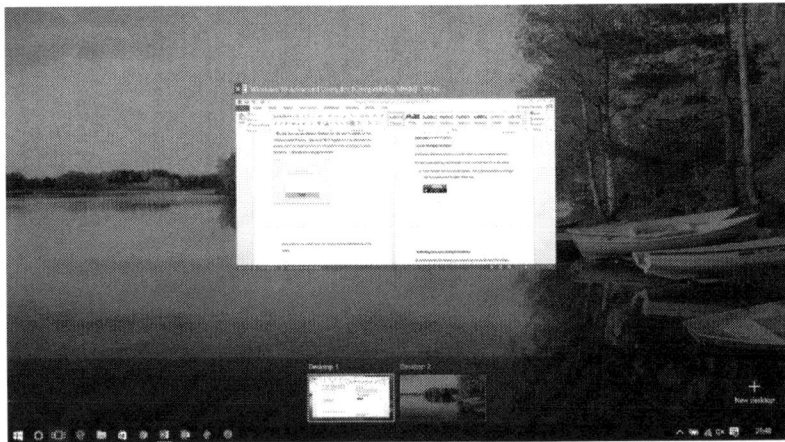

2) Press the Windows key and Tab at the same time. This launches *Task View* > Click *New Desktop* > This will automatically create a new desktop.

-Close A Desktop

To close a desktop, enter *Task View* > In the preview bar along the bottom, hover the icon of the desktop you wish to close. A small cross will appear in the top right-hand corner.

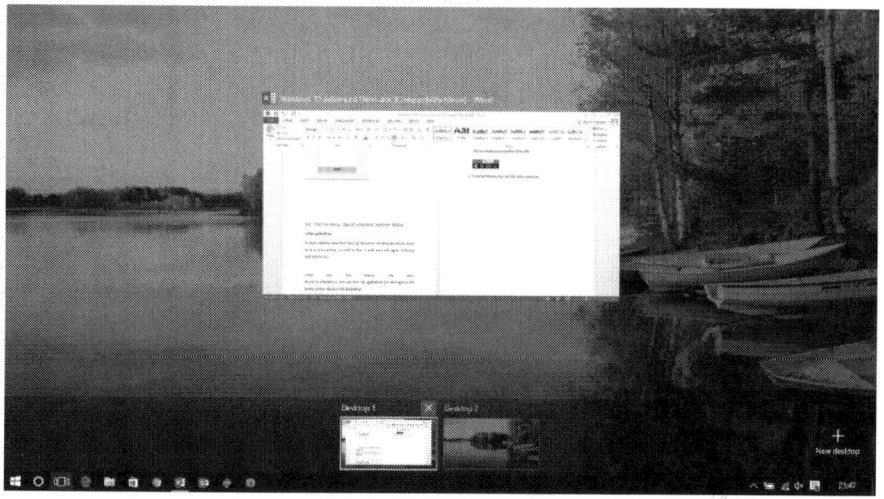

Click this. The desktop will close. Be sure to remember to save and close any applications you have open in the desktop as they will close with the desktop.

-Switching Between Multiple Desktops

To switch between the desktops you have set up you can do one of two things:

1) Press the task view icon on the taskbar. This symbol resembles a rectangle with two small square brackets on either side > Choose the desktop you want to use from the previews.

2) Press the Windows key and Tab at the same time which will bring up *Task View* > Choose the desktop you want to open.

Conclusion

It is without a doubt that Microsoft has made a big impact with the release of Windows 10. The numerous overhauls across the operating system have been a long time coming. From the initial design to everyday features like the Start Menu, Action Center, and taskbar, this operating system is arguably the most accessible of all Windows operating systems.

The addition of Microsoft Edge has brought Microsoft and Windows 10 to the forefront once again. This credible web browser, which boasts a stylish, secure, and safe internet experience rivals the current favorites.

With all the features, integrations, tricks, and innovations available with the Windows 10 upgrade it is almost like having a new computer!

Although arguably the most accessible and fluid of all Microsoft's operating systems, there are common problems that will occasionally be encountered. From blue screen errors to incorrect update installations, it's all part of the package. Microsoft has always had a strong point with quick remedies and that is no different in Windows 10.

The addition of Windows Update Delivery Optimization has been a sticking point for many Windows users with beginners feeling intimidated by the complexity of the process and advanced users concerned about security issues. We have highlighted a range of commonly asked questions and supplied you with the answers you need to decide how you can use Delivery Optimization. The same goes for Wi-Fi Sense.

Microsoft has designed Windows 10 to be customizable, in a sleek and simple manner which means there are few advanced features to customize.

All in all, the combination of a simple setup and straightforward resolution make Windows 10 an undoubtedly easy operating system to use. Added with Cortana, Windows Update Delivery Optimization, Wi-Fi Sense, and the package of ace security features there is little to pick fault in.

Windows 10 will allow the user to enjoy all aspects of daily life, personal, work, leisure, and things that just seem to pop up. The new face of Microsoft's operating system is an important piece of evolution for the computer, tablet, and phone. Expect the updates to remain free and the innovations to continue to come as Microsoft ushers in another dimension to their operating system.

Thanks for reading. I hope you enjoy it. I ask you to leave your honest feedback.

I think next books will also be interesting for you:

Amazon Tap

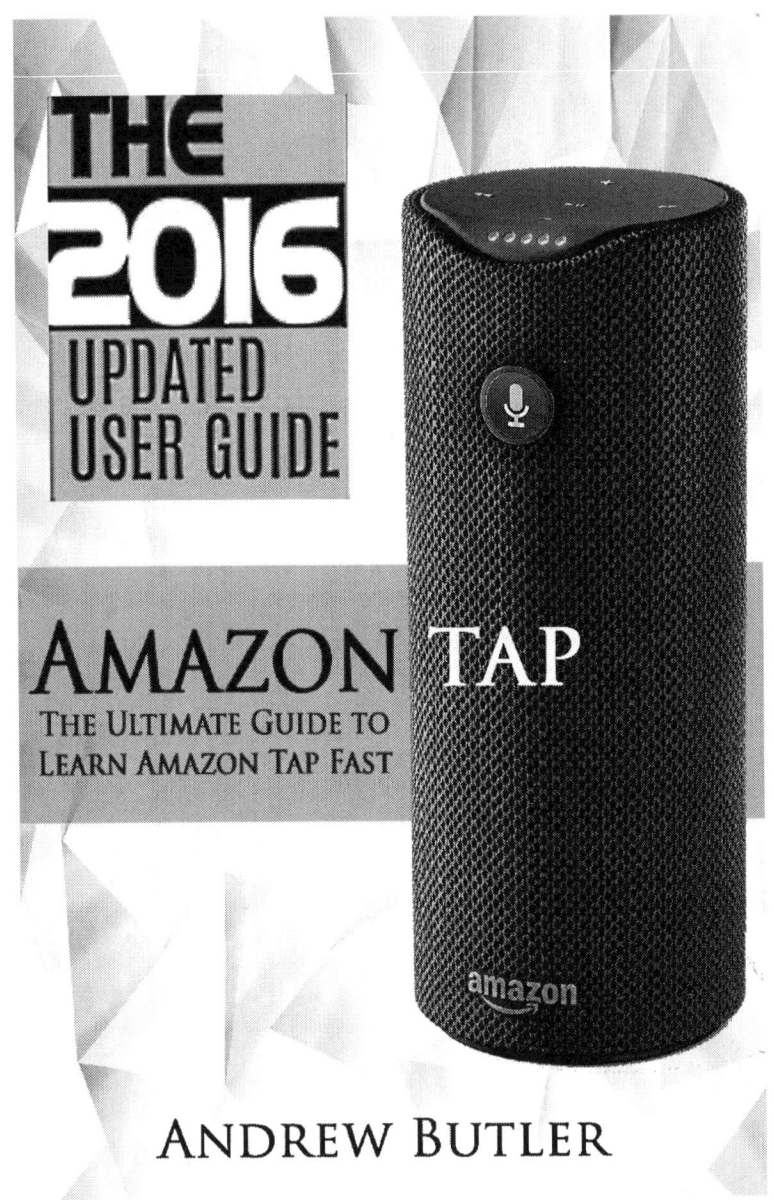

Amazon Echo

Amazon Dot

Windows 10

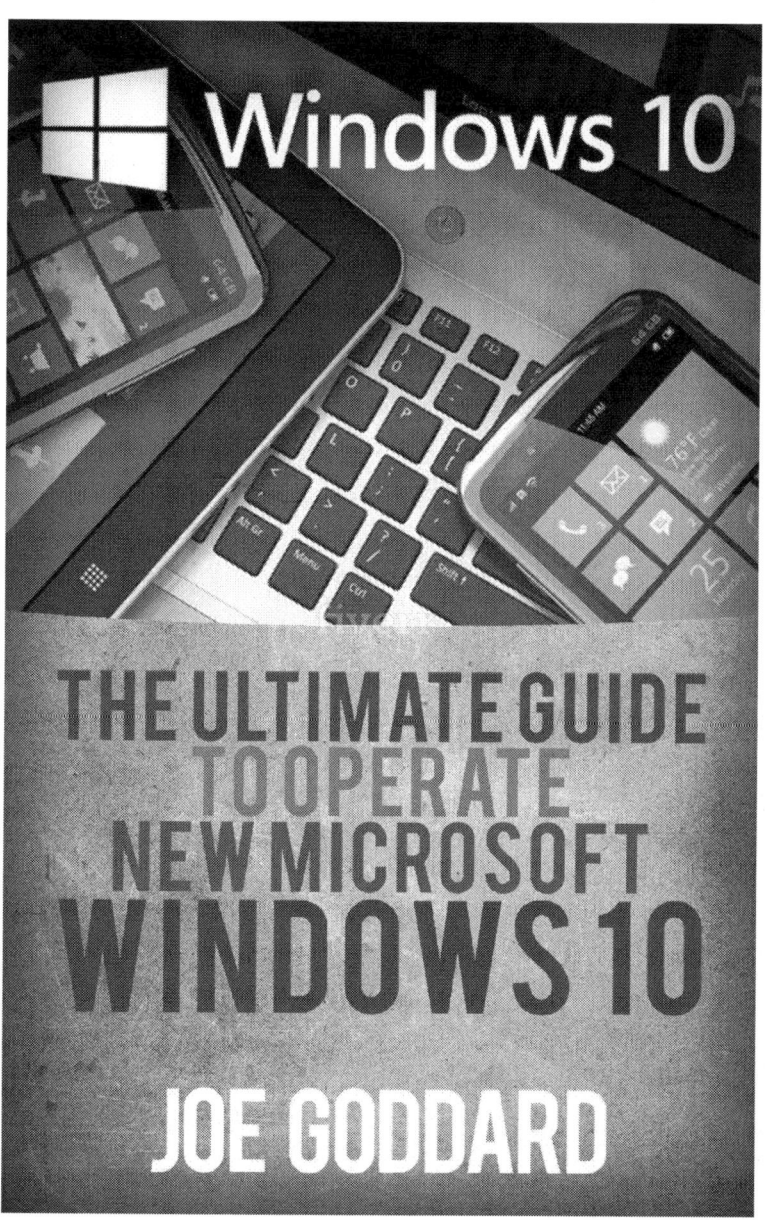

Amazon Fire TV

Amazon Echo

Printed in Great Britain
by Amazon